M000204266

# Praying the Jesus Prayer

# ☐ CHRISTIAN SPIRITUALITY SERIES ☐

# Praying the Jesus Prayer

*A Contemporary Introduction
to an Ancient Method of
Contemplative Prayer*

**Brother Ramon SSF**

Marshall Pickering

Marshall Morgan and Scott
Marshall Pickering
3 Beggarwood Lane, Basingstoke, Hants RG23 7LP, UK

Copyright © 1988 Brother Ramon SSF
First published in 1988 by Marshall Morgan and Scott Publications Ltd
Part of the Marshall Pickering Holdings Group
A subsidiary of the Zondervan Corporation

*British Library CIP Data*

Ramon, *Brother*
    Praying the Jesus prayer.
    —(Evangelical spirituality series).
    1. Prayer
I. Title   II. Series
243.3′2    BV210.2

    ISBN 0-551-01541-1

Text Set in Baskerville by Brian Robinson, Buckingham
Printed in Great Britain by Henry Ling Ltd., at the Dorset Press,
Dorchester, Dorset

# Contents

# The Name of Jesus

(Tune: Lydia C.M.)

Jesus! the name high over all,
　In hell, or earth, or sky;
Angels and men before it fall,
　And devils fear and fly.

Jesus! the name to sinners dear,
　The name to sinners given;
It scatters all their guilty fear,
　It turns their hell to heaven.

Jesus! the prisoner's fetters breaks,
　And bruises Satan's head;
Power into strengthless souls it speaks,
　And life into the dead.

O that the world might taste and see
　The riches of His grace;
The arms of love that compass me
　Would all mankind embrace.

His only righteousness I show,
　His saving grace proclaim;
'Tis all my business here below
　To cry: 'Behold the Lamb!'

Happy, if with my latest breath
　I may but gasp His name;
Preach Him to all, and cry in death:
　'Behold, behold the Lamb!'

Charles Wesley

# Foreword

The *Jesus Prayer* is a way of praying, of entering into communion with God. It is joyful and life-giving; it sustains the believer in times of discouragement and darkness; it brings the whole person into the loving awareness of God's mysterious presence. But it demands disciplined practice!

The roots of the *Jesus Prayer* are in the New Testament, and I discovered varieties of its practice within the Eastern Orthodox Churches and in the spontaneous worship of the classic pentecostal churches. As well as deepening my own life of prayer in the Holy Spirit, the *Jesus Prayer* links me with believers of the earliest New Testament days, right down through the history of the Church, to these days when Christians of all denominations are sharing together in love and prayer.

The method set out in this book is one which has been of great help to me and I have taught it to others on a personal and corporate basis. It is very simple, but at the same time profound in its form, meaning and practice. It may not be the method for everyone, and certainly it is not 'instant prayer for busy people' – there's no such thing. But it will repay the application and discipline of perseverance with spontaneity, joy and ever-deepening trust in God.

Read this book carefully, practise it prayerfully, continue with it perseveringly, and learn the 'joy unspeakable and full of glory' that comes from unceasing prayer.

Brother Ramon SSF
The Society of St Francis
Lent 1988

9

# Praying the Jesus Prayer

*Lord Jesus Christ, Son of God, have mercy on me, a sinner*

## Prayer is Communion with God

It is important that one thing is made clear at the outset. Prayer is communion, fellowship, union with God. There are no techniques, methods, exercises or forms that can manipulate or command God. Prayer is not magic, and methods are not magical formulae. God is sovereignly free, at the beck and call of no-one, and he cannot be persuaded, cajoled, bribed or enticed. The sovereignty of God is the sovereignty of Love, and therefore, God delights to draw his creatures into a loving relationship with himself, and the centre, the core of this relationship, is the practice of prayer.

Another important matter is that those who seek fellowship and union with God in prayer must be drawn into the forgiving relationship of reconciliation. God is creator and we are creatures; God is holy and we are sinful. There is the gulf of finitude and the gulf of sinfulness to be bridged, and the bridgebuilder is Christ, who is our Saviour and High Priest before the Father. By the power of the Holy Spirit, Jesus the Christ was born of the Virgin Mary, lived a life of holiness and compassion, died upon the cross as Saviour, and rose triumphant from the dead.

Therefore, the first stirring of prayer is the interior

movement of the Holy Spirit within the human heart, opening the eyes to God's presence in creation and in the redeeming work of Jesus. The believer who is thus drawn to the Father, through the Son, by the power of the Holy Spirit, is the one in whom prayer is kindled. A biblical theology of prayer is one in which both sides of the truth are acknowledged and experienced – the one side being the initiative of God, and the other, the co-operation of man. The New Testament word *synerge* (working-together) expresses the power of the Holy Spirit and the will of the believer working together for the glory of God and the benefit of man. The initiative of God is maintained and the openness of the believer is affirmed.

This principle is expounded in theology and experience throughout the New Testament, most powerfully in the life and ministry of Jesus, and consequently in the experience of the early Church.[1] Such synergism or mutual co-operation is spelled out in the words of St Paul to the Philippian believers: 'Work out your own salvation with fear and trembling; for God is at work in you, both to will and to work for his good pleasure.'[2]

## Diverse Forms of Prayer

If prayer is communion with God, and God's Holy Spirit works in mutual co-operation with the human spirit, then the forms of prayer are likely to be diverse, within the whole experience of humankind. No two congregations and no two individuals will have quite the same experience, for uniqueness is the mark of God's activity with men. In the history of the Church, corporate prayer has been experienced as both liturgical and spontaneous.

Both these forms are charismatic in different ways. The

classic liturgies of the universal Church all bear the marks of the Holy Spirit expressing the Church's confession, worship and adoration of God. Eucharistic liturgies, especially, have given rise to great poetry and great music in many languages. And spontaneous outbursts of penitence, intercession and adoration are found in every age and in every part of the Church. Together with these corporate forms of a liturgical and spontaneous character, there are the classic traditions of contemplative prayer exemplified in Benedictine, Carmelite, Ignatian, Franciscan and other devotional traditions. The contemplative life of prayer is rooted in all these traditions, and pervading all of them is a mystical sense of God's dynamic presence, for in all their diversity they belong to the one Spirit in the Unity of God's salvific dealings with humankind.

## Methods and Techniques of Prayer

Having acknowledged the diversity of prayer forms, it is not my present purpose to deal with any of the liturgical or charismatic forms of prayer which are historical or contemporary in the Church, but rather to zoom in on a particular method and technique which is native to the Eastern Churches and is proving invaluable to Christians of all confessions in these very days when there is a revival of experiential interest in the deepening of the contemplative and interior life.

I have already made it clear that there is no technique or method that can conjure up the presence and reality of God, for he is sovereignly free. But since God desires to enrich our lives with the sense of his loving presence, there are simple ways in which we can put ourselves in the way of prayer. God dwells with the humble of heart and contrite of spirit, and wherever there is a believer who in penitence and faith opens his heart to God, there God manifests his presence and power. If we want to become proficient in any of the great disciplines of philosophy, science, art or music, there must be a strength of desire, an application of mind and heart and a persistence in practice. This applies as much to learning a language as to playing an instrument. It applies also in the physical disciplines, for a sportsman must apply not only his mind but his body to exercise and practice, until he perfects his art and style. So it is with the ways of prayer. The contemplative path is one in which strength of desire, application of body, mind and spirit, and persistence in practice, become absolutely necessary for perfection in the way.

These principles are set down not for your discouragement, but to affirm that the initiative and power are with God, and therefore to encourage you, for if you have faith as a grain of mustard seed, then the Lord will do the rest, as long as your heart and mind are set upon him.

The physical and mental preparation for the saying of the *Jesus Prayer* which I shall set down is one which may be used as a preparatory form for entering into a thematic meditation, scripture meditation, or as a preparation for any meditative practice, leading to silence and resting in the presence of God. I shall use it here as a preparation for the saying of the *Jesus Prayer*, which itself will give way to a quiet resting within the divine Love. But before we begin with the matter of methods or techniques, I want to say a few things about the theology of the *Jesus Prayer*.

## Theology of the Jesus Prayer

The *Jesus Prayer* is a prayer of repetition. It is not the vain

14

repetition which is condemned in scripture, but the repetition of penitence and adoration extolled in scripture. In the prophet Isaiah's vision of the heavenly court and in the Apocalypse, the heavenly choir of cherubim and seraphim, with the whole company of heaven, cry out antiphonally and ceaselessly in words of adoration and worship, extolling God - Father, Son and Holy Spirit:

> Holy, Holy, Holy, is the Lord God Almighty,
> Who was and is and is to come.[3]

The penitential use of repetition is the calling upon God for mercy, as in the story of the penitent tax collector who went up into the temple to pray, and beat upon his breast, crying: 'God, be merciful to me, a sinner,' and in the blind man at Jericho who cried continually and persistently upon the name of Jesus for mercy and healing, much to the chagrin of the religionists in the crowd: 'Jesus, Son of David, have mercy upon me.'[4] This is not repetitive petition to one who is reluctant to forgive or heal, but the repetition of love, of praise, of worship and human need to the adorable Lord who pours his Holy Spirit into the praying heart. We shall go on to see that such praying also overflows in compassionate intercession and becomes cosmic in its scope and awareness.

Therefore the repetition is not some meaningless mantra, but it is a devotional form of words which carry precise and yet mystical, theological meaning. Every word of the *Jesus Prayer* bears witness to the fullness of the Gospel.

*Kyrios* (Lord) is the acknowledgement of the divine authority, and when linked with the name of Jesus it is the confession of the early Church, for no-one can confess that Jesus is Lord, except by the indwelling power of the Holy Spirit.[5] *Christos* is the messianic title of Jesus, the anointed One, foretold by the prophets, anointed by the Spirit with the seal of the Father's approval. He is the anointed One who brings salvation, and therefore the *Son of God*, come in power and great glory. The cry for *mercy* is the universal call from sinful and suffering humanity, and the confession of *sin* is the humble acknowledgement of human need which brings forth the divine forgiveness and redemption.

The *Jesus Prayer* is implicitly trinitarian because it acknowledges the Son as the manifestation of the Father's glory, and the power of the Holy Spirit is acknowledged in the sincere utterance of the prayer from the believing heart. Together with the biblical theology of the 'power of the Name',[6] it becomes clear that the sinner who sincerely uses the *Jesus Prayer* is one who experiences forgiveness, reconciliation with God and participation in the life of the Holy Spirit.[7] He is a reconciled sinner who pours out from a loving heart his penitence, intercession and adoration in the repetition of the *Jesus Prayer*.

## Praying the Jesus Prayer

Now we come to the matter of actually praying the prayer. This section is practical, devotional and theological. It concerns body, mind and spirit, and is divided into, (a) PRE-PARATION; (b) PRACTICE and (c) GOAL. The preparation has to do with physical relaxation, posture, breath-awareness and heartbeat; the practice is the actual saying of the prayer verbally, mentally and spiritually; the goal has to do with the aims of the prayer as it leads to deeper union with God, compassionate concern for all creatures and cosmic awareness of God's presence and love throughout the whole created order.

(a) *PREPARATION*. Choose your time wisely, at least an hour after a meal, and with an empty bladder! Remove shoes and avoid tight constrictive clothing – a track suit is ideal. Choice of place needs privacy and quiet, avoiding bright artificial light. A 'focal point' helps some people, – perhaps a candle burning before an icon, crucifix or open bible.

Now the matter of relaxation and posture. You can lie 'corpse-like' on your back upon the floor, arms stretched at sides, palms upward, or you can sit cross-legged, or upon a low stool or straight-backed chair. I usually use a prayer stool which avoids circulation-restriction to the lower limbs. Whatever the posture, keep the back straight, and begin a simple relaxation technique in talking to the members of your body, beginning at the toes, telling them gently to stretch and relax, ascending slowly from the feet, up the legs, pelvis, abdomen, chest, spine, including the hands and arms, up to the shoulders, neck and throat, and then the muscles of the jaw, face, forehead, scalp, until the whole body is gently relaxed, with no strain, no push, no sweat. It is a gentle, easy resting within the love of God, with no anxiety or worry, no tenseness, strain or holding back.

This naturally leads to breathing-awareness. When you are relaxed, the breathing will deepen and slow down somewhat, and breathing will be from the diaphragm rather than the top of the chest – belly-breathing rather than chest-breathing. Note your breathing now, and gently deepen it, breathing a little slower. Try some simple, slow-breathing, finding your own rate, centring down into a quiet and relaxed resting attitude. The word *ruach* in the Old Testament and *pneuma* in the New Testament are the words which denote spirit, wind and breath. When God breathed into the inert Adam-figure in the Genesis narrative he came to life, and when Jesus breathed on the disciples in the upper room, he breathed the breath of the Holy Spirit upon them. The wind is universal in the world, breathing is universal among men, and the Holy Spirit is the omnipresent Breath of God, breathing throughout all creation, and in your mortal body.

When you have practised simple, quiet breathing for a while, then become aware of your heartbeat. Of course this can be felt at various pressure-points over the body, but if you are quiet, relaxed and still, you should be able to feel your pulse, the beating of your heart, quietly and rhythmically within your body. You may think of this as the echo of the heartbeat of God throughout the world, for it springs from the same creative impulse that moves the sun, moon and stars, that causes the ebb and flow of the tide, the rising of the sap in springtime, and the changing of the seasons. It is a realisation, in experience, that your body is the temple of the Holy Spirit, and that the Spirit of God breathes life into your mortal body, – and this very fact glorifies God.[8]

Now this is the point at which any form of meditation may begin, – a led meditation upon a theme, a scripture meditation, meditation to music, an exercise in cosmic awareness, or the participation in an art form like painting, music, calligraphy, poetry, etc. Or this may be the point of entry into silent, imageless prayer, of resting within the divine Love, pliable in the hands of God, as clay in the hands of the potter. And this is the point at which you may begin to say the *Jesus Prayer*.

Of course, this is also the point at which somebody says to me: 'I have practised relaxation and posture – that's all helpful and good, but my problem is not getting the body quiet, it is my unquiet mind. I am troubled, distracted and bombarded by stray, adverse and very inappropriate thoughts at this point. My mind is not still, but ceaselessly active, even frantic, as if it has become afraid of the stillness of the body.' Yes, that is common, and it persists – more in some people than others. The old masters used to talk of 'the expulsive power of a new affection' – you know, if I give Mungo, our monastery dog, a bone, he will drop the cardbox box which he is carrying. I mean that if you give your mind the *Jesus Prayer* to repeat, then it will occupy itself with the prayer, – it will have something to chew upon, and you can then descend with the mind in the heart, before the Lord.

It is something like the *scuba* diver who leaves the restless surface of the ocean with its choppy waters, and descends into the depths, into a new dimension of peace and tranquillity, to new discoveries of beauty and life. So later, when you are actually praying the prayer, and find distracting thoughts invading your mind, – don't on the one hand struggle and strain *against them*, nor on the other hand let them *take possession*, but rather simply ignore them and return to the prayer, return to the prayer, return to the prayer. However many times it happens, don't get discouraged, just return to the prayer. Now let's carry out this advice into the actual practice of saying the prayer.

(b) *PRACTICE*. Remember that the words of the *Jesus Prayer* are: *Lord Jesus Christ, Son of God, have mercy on me, a sinner*. If you are saying the prayer alone, you may like to say it mentally with the rhythm of your breath, or verbally with the beating of your heart. There are various rhythms, and you can work out your own. For instance, you may like to say the prayer with the regularity of your breathing by dividing the prayer into two, and breathing in during the first half, *Lord Jesus Christ, Son of God*, and out during the second half, *Have mercy on me , a sinner*. Or you may divide the prayer into four as follows:

```
In-breath:    Lord Jesus Christ
Out-breath:  Son of God
In-breath:    Have mercy on me
Out-breath:  a sinner
```

If you would prefer to say the prayer according to the body-pulse, as I do, then it may be divided into eight, as follows:

| | | | |
|---|---|---|---|
| 1 | Lord Jesus | 5 | Have mercy |
| 2 | Christ | 6 | on me |
| 3 | Son of | 7 | a sinner |
| 4 | God | 8 | PAUSE |

If you find this too fast, you may then take each division over two beats, – this is all a matter of practice and experimentation.

## Three Stages of the Prayer

The masters of the *Jesus Prayer* in the Eastern Church speak of the three stages of the prayer, and this is an important practical and spiritual differentation. The prayer may be uttered (i) with the lips; (ii) in the mind, and (iii) in the heart, and these indicate the process of depth which is involved in the saying of the *Jesus Prayer*. It may be many years before the prayer is truly rooted in the heart, but glimpses of such deep communion with God are often vouchsafed to the believer, giving assurance of the reality and validity of such prayer.

(i) The first stage is to repeat the prayer *with the lips*. If the mind is distracted or the heart not fully set upon God, don't be anxious, just simply pray the prayer, and keep on quietly, gently, persistently. As long as there is the desire to know and love God, that is enough. The prayer will take root in its own time – in God's time.

(ii) In the second stage the lips remain closed. It is *in the mind* that the prayer is repeated. It may be that you will say the prayer with the lips one hundred or two hundred times, and then move on to the second stage. Now the prayer is repeated in the mind, but it is not so much a mental *exercise* as a simple *awareness* of the name. What I am trying to avoid is mental exertion – a sort of brain-praying! It is rather allowing the name of Jesus to wash over you, allowing the *Jesus Prayer* to repeat itself, and there is more passivity than strain to it. Allow the prayer to pray itself in and through you by the Holy Spirit. This brings us to the borders of the third stage.

(iii) Here, the Name 'descends' from the mind to *the heart* and this is another way of saying that the Holy Spirit really prays the prayer, using the believer's body, mind and spirit as an instrument of prayer, just as a flautist blows gently across his flute, and with expert fingering produces harmonious melody which delights the heart of the player and the hearers. This echoes the theology of St Paul: 'Likewise the Spirit helps us in our weakness; for we don't know how to pray as we ought, but the Spirit himself intercedes for us with sighs too deep for words. And he who searches the hearts of men knows what is the mind of the Spirit, because the Spirit intercedes for the saints according to the will of God.'[9]

This leads the believer into a process of an ever-deepening relationship and union with God. It is the depth at which contemplative prayer embraces the whole being, and in which all barriers melt in the loving presence and awareness of God's

love. St John of the Cross writes about such unitive prayer in
this way:

> How gently and how lovingly
> Thou liest awake in my bosom
> Where alone Thou secretly dwellest;
> And in Thy sweet breathing
> Full of grace and glory
> How tenderly Thou fillest me
> With Thy love.

(c) *GOAL*. It is difficult to speak of the aim or goal of such
prayer, for there is a sense in which it is a process of union
which is as infinite as it is intimate. The New Testament word
for goal, aim or end is *telos*, but it indicates *meaning* or *design*
rather than goal or end. The meaning and design of the *Jesus
Prayer* is an ever-deepening union with God, within the
communion of Saints. It is personal, corporate and eternal,
and the great mystics, in the biblical tradition, come to an end
of words. They say that 'eye has not see nor ear heard', they
speak of 'joy unspeakable' and 'groanings unutterable' and
'peace that passes understanding'.

But there are some things which we can say, which are
derivative of that central core of ineffable experience. We can
say that such prayer contains within itself a new theology of
intercession. It is not that we are continually naming names
before God, and repeating stories of pain, suffering and
bereavement on an individual or corporate level, but rather
that we are able to carry the sorrows and pain of the world
with us into such contemplative prayer as opens before us in
the use of the Jesus Prayer. God knows, loves and understands
more than we do, and he carries us into the dimension of
contemplative prayer and love, and effects salvation,

reconciliation and healing in his own way, using us as the instruments of his peace, pity and compassion.

Thus we can say that the 'prayer of the heart' unites us with the whole order of creation, and imparts to us a cosmic awareness of the glory of God in both the beauty and the sadness of the world. The process of transfiguration for the whole world has begun in the Gospel, but it will not be completed until the coming of Christ in glory. And until that time we are invited, through prayer, to participate in the healing of the world's ills by the love of God. And if we participate at such a level, then we shall know both pain and glory. The life and ministry of Jesus in the gospels reveal this dimension, for Jesus was at one and the same time the 'man of sorrows, acquainted with grief', and the transfigured healer, manifesting the glory of the Father upon the holy mountain.[10]


## Corporate Use of the Jesus Prayer

All that I have said about the *Jesus Prayer* above may be applied in group participation. Of course, it cannot then be repeated according to the breathing or heartbeat of any individual, but rather will follow the leader or officiant who will regulate the rhythmic repetition of the prayer. If this is the case then counting on a simple rope or bead rosary will indicate when a hundred (or whatever number) repetitions have been reached. Such a prayer rope (Greek *Komvoschoinion*; Russian *tchotki*) is part of the equipment of the novice in Eastern monasticism, for his watchword is the Name of Jesus. These ropes are available, or you can string a hundred beads on a cord, with one large bead to tell you when you get to the end.

I have introduced the *Jesus Prayer* to many individuals and groups of people, and frequently teach the method to groups to whom I minister or who come to the monastery for such teaching. After some instruction along the lines of this booklet, we find our place in the monastery chapel, spend some minutes in relaxation, posture, breathing, pulse-awareness and generally centring down. Then the leader will make the invocation: 'In the Name of the Father, † and of the Son, and of the Holy Spirit', and begin quietly and rhythmically to repeat the *Jesus Prayer*. It is usually said in English, though it may be repeated in Greek: *Kyrie Iesou Christou, Huie tou Theou, eleison me, ton hamartolon*. In one monastery I know it is repeated in the various languages of the participants without disorder.

After perhaps one hundred repetitions, (the first stage), the group enters into silence for an agreed period (perhaps 30–60 minutes), bearing in mind the teaching on the *stages* of the prayer. It is the Holy Spirit who enables the believer to descend from the mind to the heart, but there must be a continual gentle openness and passivity so that this can happen. During the first-stage repetition of the prayer the group may all participate verbally or may just listen and join in mentally. If the group meets together regularly, there is effected a real sense of fellowship, a corporate sense of prayer and a sharing in the embrace of God's love. It may be that the group, from time to time, may offer up such a period for a particular purpose (what used to be called a divine intention), – that of the peace and reconciliation of the world, or the blessing or healing of a person or group of persons. And, of course, any group meeting regularly to say the *Jesus Prayer* will be interested to study the theology of the prayer and the contemplative teaching of the Desert Fathers.